Looking at Plants

David Suzuki

with BARBARA HEHNER

Stoddart Young Readers

Stoddart

First published in 1985 by
Stoddart Publishing Co. Limited
34 Lesmill Road
Toronto, Canada
M3B 2T6

CANADIAN CATALOGUING IN PUBLICATION DATA

Suzuki, David T., 1936-
  David Suzuki : looking at plants

Includes index.
ISBN 0-7737-5039-8

1. Plants—Juvenile literature. 2. Botany—Experiments—Juvenile literature. I. Hehner, Barbara, 1947— II. Title.

QK49.S89 1985   J581   C85-099027-0

DESIGN: Brant Cowie/Artplus

Printed in Canada

Table of Contents

To Severn, Sarika and Joshua with love.

AN IMPORTANT NOTE FOR KIDS AND GROWNUPS
You will see this ⊘ warning sign on some of the **Things to Do** in this book. It means that an adult should help out. The project may use some boiling water or something might need to be cut with a knife. Everyone needs to be extra careful. Most grownups will want to get involved in these nature projects anyway—why should kids have all the fun?

Rules For Nature Lovers

1. Never take all the leaves and flowers from a plant. Take just what you need.

2. When you are picking a flower, break or cut the stem. Don't pull the plant up by the roots.

3. Don't taste or eat any plants, berries or seeds you find outdoors. Some plants are very poisonous. Check with an adult.

4. Don't pick a flower from anyone's garden or backyard without asking permission. Remember that in many public parks and gardens, flowers must not be picked.

5. Don't pick a wildflower if there are only a few of its kind growing where you find it. Greedy picking might mean this kind of flower will not grow in that spot anymore. Then no one else will ever be able to enjoy it again.

Introduction

My earliest childhood memories of nature are of animals—I collected insects and raised fish. I took plants for granted because they don't run or fly or sing songs. But gradually I came to love plants too. Every spring we collected flowers and edible ferns and breathed the lovely perfumes of broom and lilacs. In the autumn we collected mushrooms and went for walks to look at the fall colors.

Plants can't move around the way we do. They have had to develop all kinds of amazing ways to protect themselves from being eaten, to make more plants and to send their seeds over long distances. They are vital for all life on this planet. You can realize how important plants are by trying to imagine what our earth would be like *without* them. The air wouldn't be fit to breathe, there would be nothing to eat and the land would be just dirt or rocks. So the next time you go out, look at a flower or a tree or any other plant with new eyes. You'll find lots to surprise and interest you.

DAVID SUZUKI

Plants All Around You

Plants For Breakfast, Lunch and Dinner

How many *seeds* have you eaten today? How many *leaves* and *roots*? None? If you had corn flakes or toast for breakfast, you ate seeds. Corn flakes are made from corn, which is the seed of a plant. Bread is made from flour — the ground-up seeds of the wheat plant. If you had lettuce in a sandwich or salad at lunchtime, you ate plant leaves. If you had carrots at dinner, you ate roots.

You probably eat plant foods at every meal. They give you minerals, vitamins, sugar, fat and protein. You need to eat all these things every day to be strong and healthy. You may not notice that you are eating leaves, seeds and other plant parts. One reason is that we sometimes process plants — chopping them, grinding them, boiling them — before we use them for food. By the time we eat them, these foods don't look much like the plants they came from.

Sugar cane is a *grass* plant which only grows in countries that are hot all year round. Most North Americans have never seen it growing. We've all tasted sugar, though. Candy is mostly sugar, and sugar is also added to pies, cakes, ice cream and many other foods. It comes from the sap in the stem of a plant.

Wheat, rye, oats and corn are other grass plants that *do* grow in Canada and the United States. But unless you live on a farm, you may never see them growing in a field, rippling in the breeze. You may only see the seeds of the plant — corn, for example — or the powder ground up from the seeds — wheat flour, for instance. Flour is used to make pasta, muffins, pancakes, cakes, cookies and pie crust. All of these foods have bits of plant in them.

Fruits are easier to spot as plant foods. Oranges, apples and cherries are juicy, delicious fruits. When we eat them, they look much the same as they did when they were picked from the trees where they grew. Fruits are plants' seed containers. Often we just eat the containers and throw away the seeds. Some fruits, though, have very small seeds scattered through them. We eat the seeds along with the container. Can you think of some fruits like this?

Peas and beans are seeds. We throw away their containers (the *pods*) and eat what's inside. This is just the opposite of what we do with oranges and cherries! In fact, we hardly ever eat a whole plant. Often only one part of the plant is good for people to eat.

Carrots, beets and radishes are plant roots. We dig them up and eat them before the rest of the plant can grow very much. Asparagus and celery are *stems*. Lettuce, cabbage and spinach are leaves. We even eat some *flowers*. Cauliflower, as its name suggests, is covered with small flower buds that have just started to grow. Broccoli is covered with little green flower buds. Sometimes broccoli is picked a little late, after yellow flowers have started to appear. If you can find some broccoli that looks a bit yellow, take a look at it through a magnifying glass — you'll see the tiny petals.

Go on a plant hunt around the kitchen. (Ask permission first!) Look in the refrigerator and the cupboards. Don't forget the spice rack either. It's probably full of seeds (sesame seeds, poppy seeds, caraway seeds), leaves (bay leaves, basil, rosemary) and maybe even *bark* (cinnamon sticks are rolled-up pieces of bark). Which part of the plant did the plant foods in your collection come from — can you tell? If all the plant foods in your kitchen could begin to sprout and grow it would be a jungle in there, wouldn't it?

SWEET TREATS FROM TREES   Imagine a stack of golden pancakes topped with luscious maple syrup — yummy! Did you know that the world's whole supply of maple syrup comes from eastern Canada and the northeastern United States? Maple syrup is made by boiling the sap of the sugar maple tree until most of the water in it is boiled away. It takes about 40 L of sap to make 1 L of syrup (or about 40 gal. of sap to make 1 gal. of syrup).

How do we get the sap from the tree? The sap is food the tree made for itself in the summer. All winter, the sap is frozen inside the tree trunk. When early spring comes, the sap melts and begins to flow inside the tree. People bore small holes in the maple's trunk and collect the sap that drips out. You'll be glad to know that doing this doesn't hurt the maple tree. Less than ten percent of its food is taken, so it still has plenty for itself. In fact, some healthy sugar maple trees have been tapped every spring for almost one hundred years.

A Bowl of Seeds Please

How would you like a nice breakfast of seeds? You're not sure? It's not as strange as it sounds. Granola cereal is mostly made of seeds (some of them ground up) and it's delicious!

What you Need:

1.5 L (6 cups)   quick-cooking rolled oats
75 mL (1/3 cup)   sesame seeds
250 mL (1 cup)   wheat germ
125 mL (½ cup)   flaked coconut
125 mL (½ cup)   chopped mixed nuts (buy them at a grocery store already chopped or ask an adult to help you chop them)
150 mL (2/3 cup)   vegetable oil
125 mL (½ cup)   liquid honey
mixing bowl
mixing spoon
measuring cups and spoons
large cookie sheet
oven mitts
spatula

What to Do:

1. Preheat the oven to 120°C (250°F).
2. Mix all the dry ingredients (everything but the oil and honey) in a mixing bowl.
3. Pour the honey and the oil over the dry mix. Mix everything together.
4. ⊘ Spread the granola thinly on a cooking sheet. Put it in the oven for one hour or until it is golden brown. Every fifteen minutes, take the granola pan out of the oven with oven mitts. Turn the granola over with the spatula and put the pan back in the oven. (This way, the granola browns evenly on all sides.)
5. ⊘ Take the granola out of the oven and let it cool.
6. Store the granola in an airtight container. It is yummy served with milk as a breakfast cereal. You can also add raisins or cut-up fruit to your bowl of granola.

Candied Petals

Have you ever eaten a rose or a violet? Now you can. These make great decorations for cake or ice cream.

What You Need:

fresh rose or violet petals
1 egg
a small bowl
an egg beater
sugar
cake rack
a big jar with a tight-fitting lid

What to Do:

1. Choose petals from fresh roses or violets. (Ask permission before picking!) Do not use petals from flowers that have been sprayed with chemicals to kill bugs.
2. ⊘ Get a grownup to help you with the next step—it's tricky. Crack the egg and separate the yolk and the white. Put the white in the small bowl. (The yolk can be used for cooking.)
3. Beat the egg white until it is foamy.
4. Dip each petal in the egg white. Shake it to remove any extra egg white. Sprinkle the petal with sugar.
5. ⊘ Put the petals on a cake rack. Dry them in the oven for 15 minutes at 66°C (150°F). Store the petals in a jar with a tight-fitting lid.

Plants From the Pantry

Would you like to start your own collection of houseplants? You can grow new plants from pieces of vegetables. Here's how:

I. SWEET POTATO VINE

What You Need:

a sweet potato with lots of "eyes"
a glass
3 toothpicks

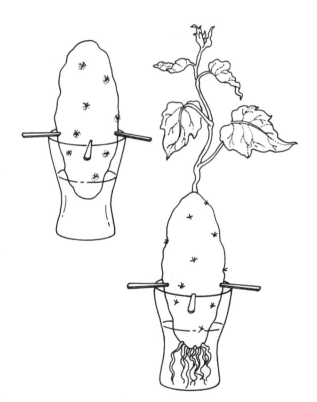

What to Do:

1. Fill the glass about half full of water.
2. Stick the toothpicks into the sweet potato like the spokes of a wheel. The toothpicks should be in the bottom third of the potato.
3. Put the sweet potato in the glass so that the toothpicks rest on the rim.
4. Put the glass in a lighted place but not in direct sunlight.
5. Keep adding water every couple of days so that the sweet potato does not dry out.
6. After three or four days, roots will begin to grow from the bottom of the sweet potato. In two or three days after that, leaves will begin to grow out of the top.
7. As the vine grows, you can train it to climb a stick or to climb up the frame of a window.

II. Carrot Plant

What You Need:
a large fresh carrot
a paring knife
a shallow dish
some small pebbles

What to Do:
1. Fill a shallow dish with small pebbles.
2. ⊘ Cut off about 5 cm (2 in.) from the big end of the carrot. Remove any leaves from the end of the carrot.

3. Place the carrot piece, cut end down, in the dish of pebbles. Put the dish in a sunny spot. Water as needed. Soon new leaves will appear from the end of the carrot.

This method also works well for turnips, beets and parsnips.

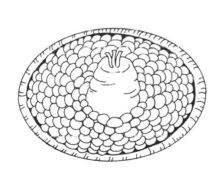

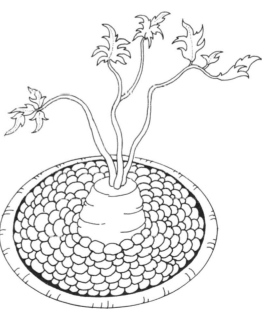

Where Would We Be Without Plants?

*H*ave you ever seen a tree house? Maybe you've seen one in a friend's backyard or in a book or on TV. It's fun to be perched up there among the leafy branches. It might get a little cramped and cold at night, though. And you certainly wouldn't want to be up there for long in the winter. It's nice to have a real apartment or house to go home to.

But guess what? Your home is a kind of treehouse too. Think about it. You are probably sleeping on trees, sitting on trees and walking around on trees. Wood is everywhere in your home — chairs, tables, floorboards, stairs, doors. It's easy to forget that all this wood came from trees. But look closely at an unpainted door. You might see the ring pattern the tree made as it grew. Sap once flowed through that wood. It was once alive.

Without trees, you wouldn't have this book to read either. Its pages are made from wood. The wood is broken down by acid to make a mushy pulp. Then it is pressed flat between huge rollers to make paper. Think of all the paper in your house right now — newspapers, magazines, books, pictures on the walls, paper towels, napkins and tissues, cardboard packaging on all kinds of things. Most of this paper came from trees. Some of the finest paper is made from cotton and linen rags rather than from wood. But cotton and linen also come from plants.

Check the labels on the clothes you have on today. Chances are good that something you are wearing has cotton in it. Cotton comes from the long soft threads attached to the seeds of the cotton plant. Linen (another fine cloth used for clothes, tea towels and tablecloths) comes from the stem of the flax plant.

Burlap is a cloth you probably wouldn't want to wear — it would be awfully scratchy. This cloth, woven from the fibers of the jute plant, is extremely strong. It's used to make sacks. If your family has ever bought a tree or a shrub from a nursery, then you have probably seen burlap sacking wrapped around the roots to protect them. Two other toughies of the plant world are hemp and sisal. Both of them are used to make very strong rope and twine.

You may never have heard of the Sapodilla tree of Central America. But you've probably tasted its sap. The sap is called *chicle* and it's used in chewing gum. The rubber tree has sap that is much less tasty but much more useful. It is made into many handy things including tires, balls and rainboots.

Plants give us some important medicines. Morphine, which is made from the poppy plant, eases severe pain; Quinine, from the bark of the Cinchona tree, is a treatment for malaria. Digitalis, a heart medicine, comes from a wildflower called foxglove.

Here are just a few more of the plant products that make our lives more pleasant. Perfume is made from flowers, herbs and spices. Shampoo and soap have plant oils in them; so does the oil paint used by artists. Many colorful dyes, including indigo (a rich purply blue), come from plants. All in all, it's hard to imagine life without the things we make from plants.

WHAT WE LEARNED FROM WASPS   For hundreds of years, people made paper from linen and cotton rags, much as we will do. As time went by, more and more books and newspapers were being printed. By the eighteenth century, there just wasn't enough cloth to satisfy the demand for paper. A Frenchman who studied insects, René-Antoine de Réaumur, noticed that wasps made their nests out of paper. The female wasps were chewing up little bits of wood until they made a mushy pulp. They spread the pulp on their nests and when it was dry — paper! Réaumur suggested that people should find some chemicals that would break down wood so that they could make paper just like the wasps did. Today's huge pulp-and-paper industry got its start because someone took a close look at some busy wasps!

Make Your Own Paper

Try making some paper from an old piece of cloth — the way paper was made for hundreds of years.

What You Need:

a piece of old white linen (perhaps
   from an old tea towel or napkin)
   15 cm x 15 cm (6 in. x 6 in.)
liquid laundry starch
a piece of wire screen (the kind
   used for window screens) about
   5 cm x 8 cm (2 in. x 3 in.)
a rolling pin
paper towels
a large mixing bowl
newspaper
water
scissors
a small saucepan
colorless powdered gelatin (buy
   this at a grocery store)
a spoon
a cup

What to Do:

1. Cut the linen into pieces about 3 cm x 3 cm (about 1 in. x 1 in.). Use your fingers to shred these pieces until you are left with a pile of threads and no cloth.
2. Pick up bunches of threads. Cut the threads into *very short* lengths.
3. ⊘ Put all the threads into the saucepan. Cover them with water. Put the saucepan on the stove and bring it to a boil. Let the thread mixture boil for ten minutes.
4. In the meantime, make some starch water. Mix 250 mL (1 cup) of laundry starch with 750 mL (3 cups) of water in the mixing bowl.
5. ⊘ Pour the boiled linen threads into the starch water. Stir them around.
6. Slide the piece of wire screen down the inside of the bowl until

it is resting on the bottom. Holding the screen flat and level, slowly lift it up. The screen should be covered with a thick layer of linen threads. If it isn't, you can shake off the threads and try it again until you are satisfied.

7. Place your screen — thread side up — on several thicknesses of paper towels. Cover with more paper towels. Roll the rolling pin over the paper towels to squeeze the water out of the threads.

8. Remove the paper towels. Put your screen—again, thread side up — on a piece of newspaper.

9. ⊘ Boil some water in a kettle or saucepan.

10. ⊘ In a cup, mix 5 mL (1 tsp.) of gelatin with 15 mL (1 tbsp.) of cold water. Stir it with a spoon until it dissolves. Then add a little boiling water to the cup until there is about 60 mL (¼ cup) of liquid. Pour about 30 mL (2 tbsp.) of this liquid over your screen of threads.

11. Let the mat of threads dry on the screen overnight. The next day, remove it carefully from the screen. There's the sheet of linen paper you have made for yourself!

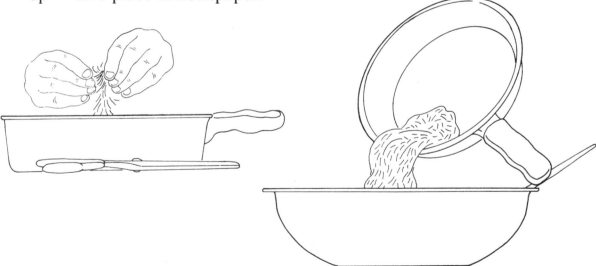

Berry Ink

This is the way ink was made by the pioneers. To use your ink, you will need a fountain pen or a straight pen. Ask your parents if they have one to lend you. If they don't, maybe they will know where to buy one in your neighbourhood.

What You Need:

ripe blueberries, blackberries, cherries or strawberries
paper cups
baby food jars or yogurt containers with lids
spoon
paper towels

What to Do:

1. Take the stems and leaves off the berries. Put the berries in a paper cup.
2. Press the berries with the back of the spoon until they are mushy.
3. Add a little water to the berries. (The more water you add, the lighter the color of the ink will be.)
4. Stir the berries and water with the spoon until they are well mixed.
5. Lay a square of paper towel over a small jar. Push the towel down into the jar.
6. Slowly pour the berry mixture through the paper towel into the jar.
7. When all the liquid has drained through the paper towel, throw the towel away. The liquid in the jar is your ink. Put the lid on the jar until you're ready to use the ink.
8. Try out different berries to see which kind makes the best ink. Is the color of the ink what you expected when you chose the berries?

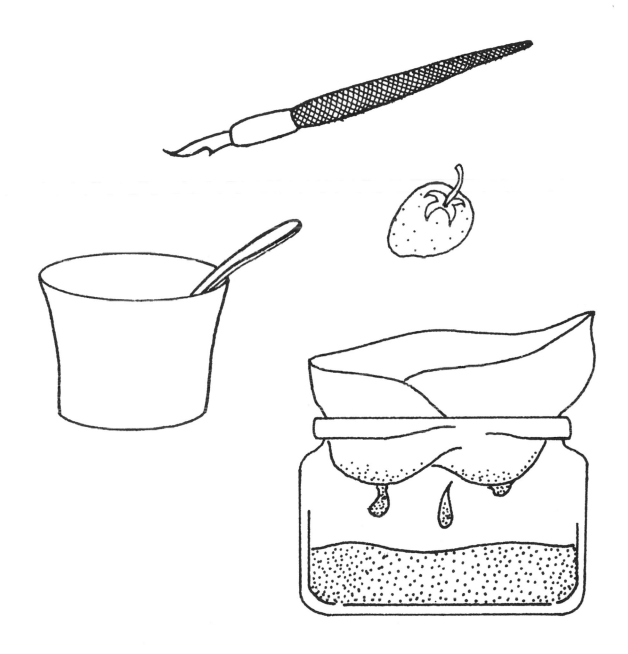

Yesterdyes

Even though most of the dyes used today are made by people, you can still dye cloth the old-fashioned way with plants. This is a big project — but fun. Ask a grownup to help you.

What You Need:

plants to use as dyes (you will need about 2 L (2 qt.) of each plant you want to use)

Here are some of the colors you can make:
yellow (onion skins)
red (stem and root of beets)
blue (blueberries)
green (stalk and leaves of lily-of-the-valley)
purple (dandelion roots)

pickling alum ⎫
          ⎬ you can buy these at a grocery store
cream of tartar ⎭

water
2 large enameled or stainless steel pots
small pieces of white cotton cloth to be dyed — hankies are just right
chopping knife and cutting board
a stirring stick
a strainer

What to Do:

Day 1

1. ⊘ Put 2 L (2 qt.) of water in one of the pots. Heat the water to boiling on the stove. Add 60 mL (4 tbsp.) of alum and 30 mL (2 tbsp.) of cream of tartar to the water. (This mixture is called *mordant.* It will help the dye to color the cloth.)
2. ⊘ Drop the piece of cloth to be dyed into the pot. Let the mordant simmer for one hour (this means just barely bubbling). Stir it once in a while.
3. Let the cloth sit in the mordant overnight.
4. While the cloth is in the mordant, you can start making the dye. Use the cutting board to chop the plants you are using for dye.
5. Put the chopped-up plants in the second pot. Add just enough water to cover them. Let this pot stand overnight too.

Day 2

1. ⊘ Let the dye pot simmer for one hour. Then strain the dye through the strainer. This gets rid of all the plant pieces.
2. Take the piece of cloth out of the mordant. Wring it out over the sink. Then put it in the dye pot.
3. ⊘ Bring the dye pot to a boil. Let it simmer for one hour. Every 10 minutes or so, use the stirring stick to push the cloth around.
4. ⊘ After one hour, turn off the stove. Take the pot to the sink. Lift out the cloth with a stick and rinse it under the cold water tap.
5. Hang the cloth to dry in a warm, dry place. It will be a very soft, pretty color.

Plants Up Close

Roots and Stems: Pipelines for Plants

*I*magine you're standing in one spot and you can't move. In fact, your feet are buried in the ground. The sun is beating down on your head. Pretty soon, you're going to get very thirsty. But you can't go anywhere to get yourself a drink.

This is just the way it is for most plants. While animals walk, run, hop, swim, slither and fly from place to place, a plant stays in one spot all its life. It is held there by its root — a part of the plant that is buried in the ground. Roots keep plants from being blown away in the wind. If you've ever tried to pull up a dandelion, you know how well anchored in the earth a root can be.

A root is much more to the plant than an anchor, though. The root gives the plant that drink it needs. Water in the soil enters the root and is carried up through the root, into the stem and out to the plant's leaves and flowers. In the water are dissolved minerals that the plant needs to grow. (When you add a spoonful of salt to a glass of water, it *dissolves*. It's still there — taste the water! — but you can't see it.)

The root is so important to the plant that it is the first part to grow when a seed sprouts. The growing tip of the root is protected by a *root cap*. The moist root cap slips easily among the soil particles. As roots branch out and spread through the ground, they make a web that holds the soil together.

There are two main kinds of roots. *Fibrous roots* are thin and have many branches. If you pull up a fistful of grass (ask permission first!), you'll see fibrous roots. *Tap roots* are large thick roots with fine roots called *root hairs* branching off them. Many tap roots act as food storage bins — and that food is good for us to eat too. Carrots, parsnips and beets are tap roots. We pull them up before the plant has a chance to use the stored food to make leaves, flowers and seeds.

How does the food get down to the roots to be stored? It travels through the stem. While water and minerals are going *up* the stem to the leaves, sugary food made by the leaves is going *down* the stem to all parts of the plant. All this liquid flowing through the plant is called sap. Sap keeps the plant alive the way blood flowing through your body keeps you alive.

You are held upright by a column of bones—your spine. A plant is held upright by its stem. The stem is not kept stiff by bone, though, but by water (just as you can make a balloon round and firm by filling it with water or air). A plant that needs a drink will often droop and fall over. After it is watered, it will soon stand straight again. Stems hold up the flowers and leaves where they can get the air and sunlight they need.

VIGOROUS VINES   Lots of movies would end in the middle if the hero or heroine didn't escape from the bad guys by swinging away on a vine. Although the vines seen in movies are pretend ones, there really are vines strong enough to swing on. They're called *lianas*. They grow in the jungles of Africa and South America. Lianas will climb a 60 m (200 ft.) tree to get to the air and sunlight they need. They're so strong that they can hold up giant trees which have died and would have fallen over without the vine's support!

A ROOT THAT'S HARD TO BELIEVE   A rye plant — a kind of grass plant — has over 13 million roots. Each of these roots, in turn, is covered with fine branching root hairs — perhaps 14 billion of them. If you could place them all end to end, they would stretch about 20,000 km (over 12,000 miles). But the rye plant has them all packed together in about 0.5 m³ (a bit less than 2 cu. ft.) of earth!

HOW BIG CAN A TAP ROOT BE?   A really big carrot from the grocery store probably weighs less than a kilogram (2 lb.). (You can find out for yourself with a kitchen or grocery store scale.) Can you imagine a tap root more than 13 times as big as that carrot? One kind of morning glory, the wild potato, has a tap root that weighs almost 14 kg (30 lb.) — and it's edible! The wild potato was an important food for the Indians and the early European settlers of North America.

Soil Savers

Let's look at the way roots can hold soil together.

What You Need:

a glass jar
water
a package of radish or mustard
  seeds
2 paper cups
about 500 mL (2 cups) rich soil

What to Do:

1. Put six seeds in the jar. Cover them with water for two or three days. They will begin to sprout. (Now they're called *seedlings*.)
2. Put soil in the two paper cups. Fill each cup until it is three-quarters full.
3. Plant three seedlings in each cup. Let them grow for two weeks. Water them a little each day — just enough to keep the soil moist.
4. After two weeks, peel away the cups from the soil. What do the roots look like? What shape does the soil have? Does this show you why we need plants to keep soil from blowing away?

Sluuurp!

Can roots and stems really pull water up into the plant? Let's find out.

What You Need:

a large, fresh celery stalk with
    several leaves attached
a large carrot
2 jars or drinking glasses
red or blue food coloring
paring knife

What to Do:

1. ⊘ Cut about 2 cm (1 in.) off the bottom of the celery stalk. Cut about 2 cm (1 in.) off the narrow end of the carrot.
2. Put water in the jars to a depth of about 5 cm (2 in.).
3. Color the water with food coloring. (The water should be *dark* blue or red.)
4. Put the celery stalk, cut end down, in one jar. Put the carrot, cut end down, in the other jar.
5. Let them stand for twenty-four hours.
6. Let's look at the celery first. What has happened to the leaves at the top of the celery? How do you think this happened?

7. ⊘ Take the celery stalk out of the water. Make a cut across the celery stalk about 2 cm (1 in.) above the first cut. What do you see inside the celery? Can you tell where the water went up the stalk?

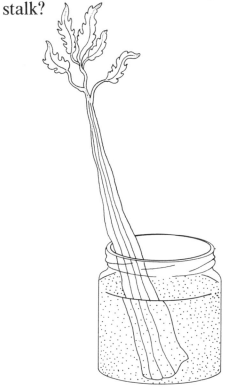

8. ⊘ Now gently scrape the length of the celery stalk with the knife. As the outer layer of the celery comes off, you can see the colored tubes running right up the celery stalk.

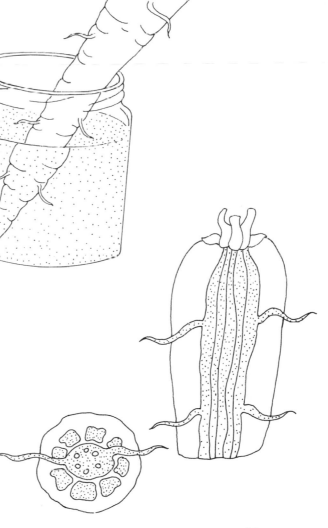

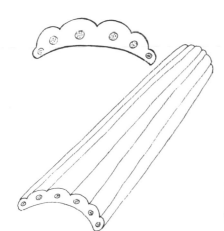

9. ⊘ Now take a look at the carrot. Cut across the end of the carrot about 5 cm (2 in.) above the earlier cut. What part of the carrot is colored? Make a cut along the length of the rest of the carrot. What do you see? Can you tell which part of this root carries water and food up to the plant?

Grow a Tasty Root

Ground ginger is sold in the spice section of most grocery stores. But fresh chopped ginger root is even yummier. You can grow your own ginger root so that you always have some for your favorite recipes.

What You Need:

a piece of fresh ginger root (sold in oriental grocery stores — some supermarkets sell it too)
a 30 cm (12 in.) flower pot
potting soil   (rich soil for house plants — sold in garden shops)

What to Do:

1. Fill the flower pot with soil. (Leave some room at the top for watering.)
2. Plant a flat piece of ginger root so that it is half-buried in the soil.
3. Keep the soil moist. Put the pot in a place that is well-lighted but out of direct sun.
4. Green *shoots* will soon start to grow out of the top surface of the root. (And thin roots are growing under the soil where you can't see them.) The green shoots look like grass and smell gingery. They may grow as tall as 1.5 m (5 ft.).
5. ⊘ After a few months, the original root will begin to grow new fat, bulging parts. Dig the root up and slice off some of this new section. (What kind of root is ginger — a tap root or a fibrous root? How can you tell?)
6. Wash the piece and chop it up for any recipe that uses ginger. Here is a delicious hot drink to get you started:

Ginger Tea

750 mL (3 cups) water
5 cm (2 in.)   fresh grated ginger
15 mL (1 tbsp.)   honey
½ sliced lemon
a saucepan
a strainer or sieve

Mix these ingredients and boil them in a saucepan for ten minutes. Strain the tea through a sieve or strainer and serve it in mugs.

Roots and Stems
in Action

What do you think would be strong enough to make a sidewalk crack? Maybe a heavy truck rolling over it? Maybe a big tree falling on it? Would you believe a plant root? The growing roots of small weeds such as dandelions have been known to push through a cement sidewalk. Tree roots clinging to cliffsides have forced their way into granite, a very hard kind of rock.

Although most plants stay in one spot, their roots and stems grow and move. As they grow, they change direction in reaction to the world around them. These plant movements are called *tropisms*. You can't see tropism movements by watching a plant — they happen too slowly. But if you go away and come back in a couple of days, you can see that a plant has been on the move.

Have you ever wondered what would happen if a seed were planted upside down? Would the stem grow down and the root grow up? No — the plant has a way to keep this from happening. A plant can feel the pull of *gravity* just as you can. (This is the force that holds you on the earth and keeps you from flying off into space.) A root always grows in the direction of the pull of gravity, toward the center of the earth. This is called *geotropism* (from the Greek word for earth).

Plant movements are also affected by water. This is called *hydrotropism* (from the Greek word for water). In a way that we don't fully understand, roots can sense where water is and usually head right for it. Roots sometimes cause trouble for us by wrapping themselves around sewer pipes — they're trying to get at the water inside.

Just as roots will grow toward water, stems will grow toward light. This is called *phototropism.* Can you guess where this word comes from? Do you know any other "photo" words?

Many plant stems show another interesting kind of movement called *thigmotropism.* The kinds of plants we call *vines* — including cucumber and bean plants — are not strong enough to stand up by themselves. They need something to hold onto. They send out thin strands from their stems called *tendrils.* Tendrils curl around fences, sticks and other supports. Somehow, without eyes, plants sense when something is nearby that their tendrils can grab — and they grab that something!

SEEDS IN SPACE   What do you think happens when seeds sprout in space where there is no gravity? Thanks to the United States space shuttle, we now know for sure. While the shuttle is in orbit, all the things inside it are weightless because gravity is not pulling them down. Scientists on the shuttle tried sprouting some seeds. (Their project was similar to the one we will do on page 39.)   Although the seeds grew roots, the roots pointed in every direction!

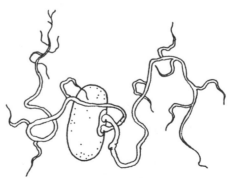

BEWARE OF THE STRANGLER!   Actually, you don't have to worry about the strangler fig tree—it only attacks other trees. The strangler fig's seeds will not sprout in the ground. They can only sprout on another tree, where they are probably dropped by a passing bird. This unlucky tree is called the "host" tree, although it certainly doesn't welcome its sinister guest. The seed grows strong thick roots that travel down the host tree's trunk to the ground. These roots send out other side-branching roots that surround the tree and gradually squeeze it to death. In the meantime, the stem and branches of the strangler fig grow very tall. They block the host tree's leaves from the sunlight. Finally the host tree dies and rots away inside its prison of roots and stems.

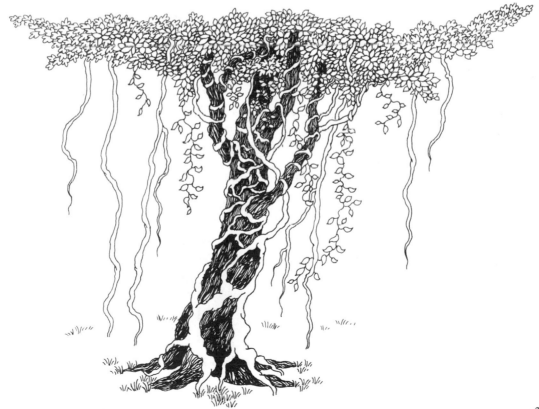

Root Power

Find out just how strong growing roots are.

What You Need:

package of small seeds (marigold
    seeds have an interesting shape
    and sprout quickly)
an eggshell, broken into two halves
2 egg cups
a tinfoil pie plate
potting soil

What to Do:

1. Fill both half-eggshells with soil almost to the top. Leave a little space at the top for watering.
2. Sprinkle seeds across the top of *one* half-eggshell. Cover the seeds with soil. (Follow the directions on the seed package for how deep they should be.)
3. Set the half-eggshells in egg cups to hold them steady. Put the egg cups on the pie plate so that you don't make a mess when you water them.
4. Treat the other half-eggshell the same way even though it has no plants in it.
5. Place the plate in the sunlight. Wait for the seedlings (the new little plants) to appear in one of the half-eggshells. Water very lightly. (Don't let the soil get soggy.) Once the seedlings are growing, you can use a little more water. If a little plant comes up in the other half-eggshell (it might have been in the soil you used), pull it out.
6. In four or five weeks, you will see one of the half-eggshells beginning to crack. Which one? Slowly, as the days go by, it will fall apart. How is the other one? Take a closer look at the broken half-eggshell and what was inside it. What do you think broke it apart? Can you see why plants sometimes cause problems for sidewalks and house foundations?

The Right Root Route

Will roots always point down, no matter which way a seed is turned?

What you Need:

a large jar
colored paper towels (roots
   show up better against a
   colored background)
bean seeds

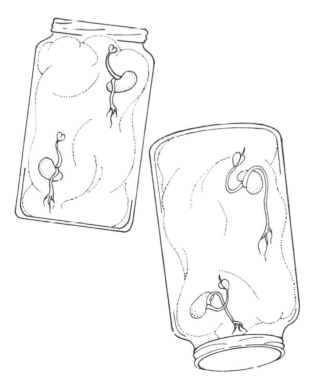

What to Do:

1. Wet some paper towels. Crumple them up and fill the jar with them.
2. Place some bean seeds between the paper towels and the side of the jar. The bean seeds should be at least 5 cm (2 in.) apart. They can be pointed in any direction.
3. Keep the paper towels moist as the bean seeds begin to sprout.
4. After three or four days, roots will be growing. Which way are they pointing? Check them again at the end of a week. Does the position of the seed make any difference to the direction the roots grow?
5. Wait until the roots are about 3 cm (1 in.) long. Then turn the jar upside down.
6. After three or four days, check the roots again. Which way are they pointing now?

SOMETHING TO DO

A Root March to Water

Find out whether roots really *will* head for water.

What You Need:

a large clear glass baking pan
a small clay flower pot
potting soil
lima beans

What to Do:

1. Fill the glass pan with potting soil.
2. Place the plant pot near one corner of the pan.
3. Plant two or three seeds about 5 cm (2 in.) away from the plant pot. Plant two or three more seeds about 10 cm (4 in.) away from the plant pot. Finally, plant two or three seeds at the far end of the pan away from the plant pot.
4. Fill the flowerpot with water. Do not water the seeds in any other way. The only water the plants will have is what seeps through the plant pot.
5. In a couple of days, seeds will begin to *germinate* (sprout). Which ones sprout first? Which ones sprout last? Why?
6. ⊘ After two weeks, check the roots. In which direction are they growing? (You can carefully pick up the glass pan — or ask a grownup to do it for you if it is too heavy — and look at the roots from underneath.)
7. After three or four weeks, what is happening around the base of the plant pot? Why do you think it happened?

A-Maze-ing Bean Plants

How many twists and turns will a plant take to get to sunlight? Build a plant maze and see for yourself.

What You Need:

dried beans
cardboard carton with dividers and
   lid (you can get this at a grocery
   store)
small flower pot
potting soil
freezer tape

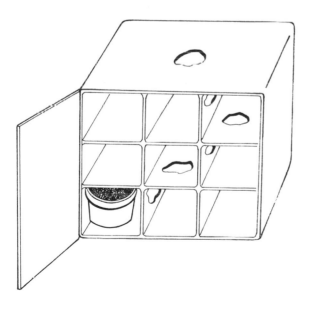

What to Do:

1. ⊘ Cut holes in the dividers of the carton to make a maze (see the drawing). The holes should be about 5 cm (2 in.) in diameter.
2. Plant four dried beans in a small flower pot. Place the pot in a corner of the carton as far away from the outside hole as possible.
3. For two weeks, keep the carton tightly sealed so that no light can get in through the lid. You might need to wrap freezer tape around the lid to keep the light out.
4. Every two or three days, open the carton to water the beans.
5. After a few days, what do you see happening?

Leaves: All Shapes and Sizes

The first day of spring, according to the calendar, comes around March 21. For many of us, though, spring really arrives when fresh green leaves appear on the trees. They have been quietly unfolding, day by day. But the wonderful moment when we *notice* them comes all at once. It seems as if yesterday the trees were bare and today they're leafy.

Leaves come in many shapes and sizes. They can be long and narrow, like weeping willow leaves. They can be almost round, like aspen leaves. They may look a little like your hand with its fingers spread, like maple leaves. Some of the prettiest leaves are made up of little leaflets joined to a stalk, like sumach leaves. It's fun to collect as many different kinds of leaves as you can. On page 45, you can learn how to press your leaf collection.

Leaves have a network of veins running through them. The veins carry water and minerals from the root and stem to the leaves. They also carry food that the leaves make to the rest of the plant. Some leaves have one main vein with smaller veins branching off. Other leaves have several main veins that spread out like a fan. Look at some leaves to see what vein patterns you can find.

When we think about leaves, we may forget that evergreen needles and cactus spines are leaves too. Evergreen needles are thick and tough and stay alive right through the winter. Sharp cactus spines protect the plant from creatures who might eat it.

In some plants, leaves have taken over jobs we might expect other plant parts to do. A tendril of a climbing vine is a special kind of leaf that acts more like a stem. Some plants have small flowers with brightly coloured leaves around them. These special leaves are called *bracts*. The bracts do the job of attracting insects to the flower. Poinsettias, which are popular plants at Christmas, have this kind of bract.

Bulbs are tightly packed bundles of leaves that act like roots. They are found below the ground, just above the real roots of the plant. Like many roots, they store food for the plant over the winter. Onions are bulbs. Many spring garden flowers, such as daffodils and tulips, are grown from bulbs.

✿ *CAN A PERSON FLOAT ON A LEAF?* The queen-size royal waterlily, which grows in Brazil, has leaves over 2 m (about 8 ft.) across. The leaves will hold up to 23 kg (50 lb.). A child could sit on one of these leaves without sinking it — but an adult would be too heavy. Although

the flat top of the leaf would make a comfortable seat, the underside would not. It's covered with sharp spines to keep fish from eating it. Waterlily leaves — usually called lilypads — float on the tops of ponds and lakes. There they can get the air and sunlight they need to make food. Far below, the root of the plant is anchored in the bottom of the lake.

POISON BUTTERFLIES The leaves of the milkweed plant are poisonous to most animals. But the caterpillars of the monarch butterfly stuff themselves with milkweed leaves — in fact, they eat nothing else. By the time the caterpillars change into butterflies, they are so full of milkweed poison that they become poisonous too. Other animals know that the beautiful orange and black butterflies are too dangerous to snack on — so monarchs are protected from being eaten.

Pressed for Time

You can take this leaf and flower press with you on a nature walk so that you can press flowers before they wilt.

What You Need:

2 pieces of heavy cardboard, about 30 x 46 cm (12 in. x 18 in.) — sides of cardboard cartons would work well (ask a grownup to help with cutting through the cardboard)
a pair of long shoelaces
scissors
felt pens in several colors
paper towels

What to Do:

1. ⊘ Use the point of the scissors to make a hole in each corner of a piece of cardboard. Make the holes at least 5 cm (2 in.) in from the edge so that the cardboard won't tear.

2. Lay the piece of cardboard with the holes over the second piece of cardboard. Use a felt pen to mark through the holes in the top piece. In this way, you can make sure that the holes in the two pieces of cardboard line up.

3. Thread the shoelaces through the holes as shown in the drawing. Decorate the outside of your press with the felt pens.

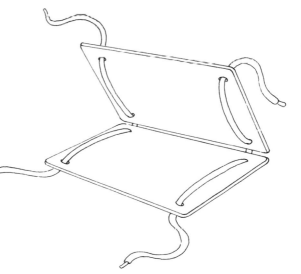

4. Put about four paper towels inside your press.

5. To press flowers and leaves, lay them flat between the layers of paper towels. Arrange them carefully. They will dry exactly as you place them on the paper.

6. Put leaves and flowers of the same thickness together. Flowers with very thick centres or stems will not press well. (Use the method on page 65 for drying them instead.) Tie up the shoelaces to hold the press closed.

7. When you get home, take out the paper towels, leaves and flowers from the press. Put them under a heavy book until they are dry. This will take about two or three days for thin leaves and flowers. It might take two weeks for large thick leaves and flowers.

Leaf Skeletons

When the rest of the leaf is removed, leaf veins make beautiful lacy designs. These delicate shapes look very pretty in dried flower arrangements.

What You Need:

some large leaves with heavy veins
   (maple leaves, for example)
a large soup pot
washing soda } buy these at a
bleach } grocery store
kitchen cutting board
an old toothbrush
paper towels

What to Do:

1. ⊘ Bring to a boil 2 L (2 qt.) of hot water. Add 30 mL (2 tbsp.) of washing soda.
2. ⊘ Add the leaves to the pot and let them simmer (just barely boil) for thirty minutes.
3. Let the water cool. Drain the water from the leaves. Then rinse the leaves gently in cold water. Drain the leaves again.
4. Spread the leaves on the cutting board. Use the toothbrush to brush away the leaf parts, leaving only the veins — the leaves' "skeletons." Be patient and work slowly and carefully.
5. ⊘ If you wish, you can bleach your leaf skeletons (make them white). Put them in a bowl containing 1 L (1 qt.) of water and 30 mL (2 tbsp.) of bleach. Leave them for one hour. Pour off the liquid and rinse the skeletons in cold water.
6. Spread the leaves on paper towels to absorb the water. Now you can press them with a heavy book. Drying will take about three or four days.

Make a Leaf Cast

You can make permanent copies of your favorite leaves using plaster of Paris.

What You Need:

a leaf with an interesting pattern
plaster of Paris
a shallow dish that is bigger than
    your leaf (the lid of a cottage
    cheese container works well)
vaseline
water
a jar
an old spoon

What to Do:

1. Lay the leaf on the dish with the underside (the veined side) facing upwards.
2. Rub a little vaseline on the leaf.

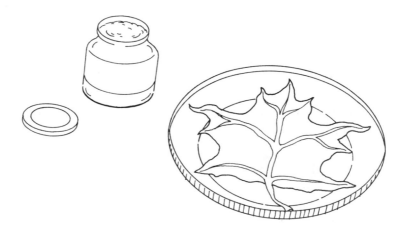

3. Put a little water in the jar. Carefully spoon plaster of Paris into the jar. Stir the mixture with a spoon. Keep adding plaster of Paris little by little until the mixture is like toothpaste.

4. Carefully spread the plaster over the leaf so that is is evenly covered. Then fill the dish with the rest of the plaster of Paris. Work as quickly as you can.

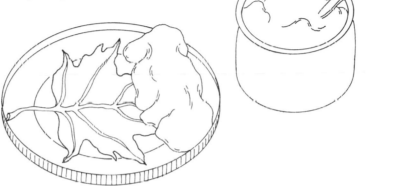

5. Leave the plaster to dry. This will take about half an hour.

6. When the plaster has hardened, you can lift it out of the dish. Carefully peel off the leaf. There in the plaster is a cast of your leaf.

Leaves in Action

All green plants — even that straggling little weed poking up through the driveway where nobody wants it — can do something truly amazing. It is something that no other living things on earth can do. They can make food just from air, water and sunlight. All animals — and that includes us — live either by eating plants or by eating animals that eat plants.

Leaves are plants' food factories. To make food, they need *carbon dioxide* — a gas that is in the air and is poisonous to animals. They also need water — which they usually get from the soil — and sunshine.

Green plants have a special chemical in their leaves called *chlorophyll*. Chlorophyll lets the plant use energy from the sunlight shining on its leaves to make food out of carbon dioxide and water. The green color of the leaves lets you know that food-making is going on. It is chlorophyll that makes leaves green.

A plant's way of making food is called *photosynthesis*. (The word comes from two Greek words. *Photo* means light and *synthesis* means putting things together in a new way.) So, plants that are getting sunlight are able to make a new thing — food.

The food plants make is a kind of sugar. Later, plants might use this sugar to make other kinds of food. Different plants do different things with their sugar. That is why we need to eat lots of different kinds of plants to have a balanced diet. While the plant is making food it is also making *oxygen*, a gas which it lets go into the air. Animals need oxygen to breathe.

Plants also use their leaves the way we use our lungs — to breathe in and out. Plants breathe through little holes on the underside of their leaves. These holes are too small for you to see, though, unless you look at a leaf through a microscope.

Think about the smoke, the noise, the smells that come from some of the factories where people make things. Then think about plant leaves — busy making food to feed the world without a sound, without any fuss at all — and cleaning the air for us at the same time!

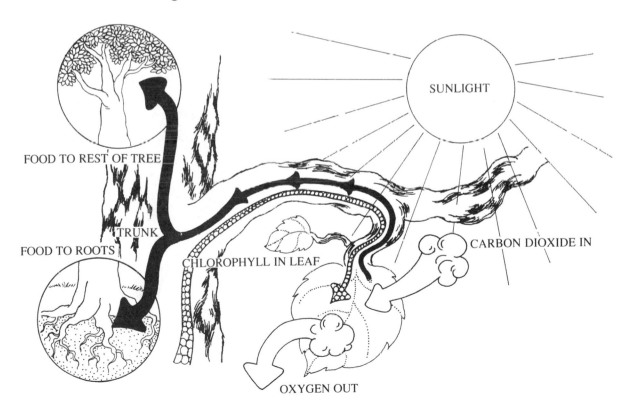

KILLER LEAVES   Killer leaves? It sounds like something out of science fiction. But there really are plants that use their leaves to catch and kill insects. Most of these plants live in bogs where the soil isn't very good. They've invented some amazing ways to spice up their diets!

The pitcher plant's leaves take the shape of deep containers where pools of water collect. Insects are attracted to the plant by its smell. But they often fall into the "pitchers" and drown. Then the plant digests them.

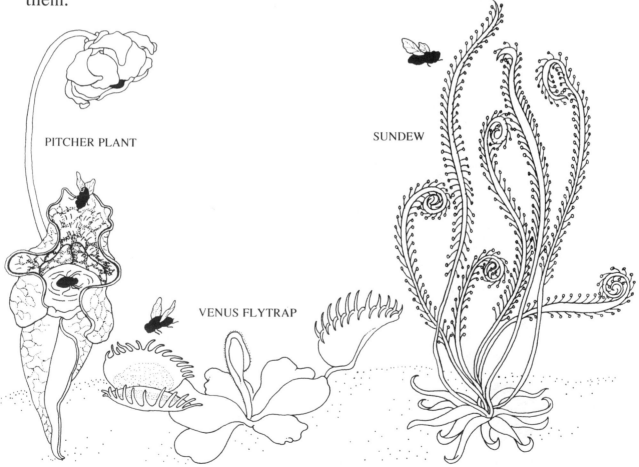

PITCHER PLANT

SUNDEW

VENUS FLYTRAP

Sundews have bright red leaves covered with hairs and a sweet sticky liquid. Insects' feet get stuck to some of the hairs on the leaf. Then the nearby hairs bend toward the insect, surround it and suffocate it.

The leaves of the Venus flytrap have a hinge right down the central vein. The leaves have special hairs that are sensitive to the slightest pressure. When an insect lands on a leaf and touches at least two of these hairs — SNAP! the leaf closes on the insect in less than a second. If only one hair is touched, nothing happens. That's so wind and raindrops won't cause it to close for nothing. When it has captured something, the trap stays closed for about a week. When it opens again, nothing is left of the unlucky insect but its skeleton.

✿ *WHY DO LEAVES CHANGE COLOR IN THE FALL?* In many parts of North America, we look forward to the brilliant colors of autumn leaves. Why do trees put on this beautiful show? It's a sign that they're getting ready for winter. We have to change our ways when winter comes, trading bathing suits for snowsuits. Trees have to change too. In the fall, as the weather grows colder, tree roots have a harder time getting water. The tree also gets less sun as the days get shorter. It is time for it to shut down its leafy food factories for the winter. The tree forms a little layer of cork at the end of each leaf stalk. As the leaf is cut off from water, it stops making food, and its chlorophyll breaks down. When the green chlorophyll is gone, you can see other colors — yellow, orange, red — that were in the leaf all along, but hidden. Eventually the stems of the leaves break right away from the tree. The leaves flutter to the ground.

Let The Sunshine In

This activity lets you see how leaves look when they are getting sunshine and how they look when they aren't.

What You Need:

small pieces of black construction
   paper
paper clips
a growing plant that has large leaves
   (a philodendron, for example)

What to Do:

1. Cut three small circles in the construction paper.
2. Attach the paper to a leaf of the plant with a paper clip. Be careful not to harm the leaf. Just three small circles of the leaf should show through the paper "mask."
3. Leave the paper attached for two days.
4. When you remove the paper mask, what do you see? Which part of the leaf is green? What color is the rest of the leaf?
5. Which part of the leaf used sunshine to make food? How can you tell?
6. Look at the leaf two or three days after the mask is taken away. What is it like now? What has happened to it?

Do Plants Really Breathe?

Leaves have tiny air holes on their surfaces. What happens to a leaf when these holes are clogged?

What You Need:

a healthy plant with lots of leaves
  (an ivy plant, for example)
a tube of vaseline

What to Do:

1. Carefully cover both sides of two leaves with vaseline. Then coat just the top side of another two leaves with vaseline and just the underside of two more leaves.
2. Give the plant the water and sunshine it needs. Look at the plant each day. How do the coated leaves look? What color are they?
3. How many days does it take before a leaf drops off? Which one is it? What happens to the leaves that have only one side coated? Why were some of these leaves able to survive?
4. What do you think happened to the leaves that were coated with vaseline?

Make a Bottle Garden

Now that you've learned a little about plants, you might like to plant some and watch them grow. You don't need much room for a garden if you plant it in a bottle. Here's how.

What You Need:

a large clear glass bottle or jar with a lid (a wide-mouthed jar is easiest to work with)

a few small green plants (you need plants that will grow slowly and stay small such as maidenhair and bracken ferns, miniature ivy and mosses

small pebbles

some charcoal briquettes

a plastic bag

a hammer

a strainer

potting soil

a piece of stiff paper

newspaper

What to Do:

1. Wash your bottle carefully with water and detergent. Rinse it very well and let it dry
2. Spread out some newspapers to make a work surface.
3. Wash any dirt off your pebbles. Put two layers of pebbles in the bottom of your bottle. Your pebble layer should be about 2-3 cm (1 in.) deep.
4. ⊘ Break up the charcoal into small pieces. Here is a tidy way to do it. Put the charcoal into a plastic bag and break it up with a hammer. Ask a grownup to do this for you. Pour the charcoal into a strainer and wash it under the tap.
5. Put one layer of charcoal into the bottle on top of the pebbles. Your charcoal layer should be about 1.5 cm (½ in.) deep.
6. Make a funnel by rolling a piece of paper. (See the drawing.) Put the funnel into the bottle. Pour the potting soil through the funnel. This keeps the sides of your bottle from

getting dirty. You will need about 5 cm (2 in.) of soil.

7. Here's how to plan your garden. On a piece of paper, draw a circle that is the same size as your garden. Arrange the plants on the paper. When you are happy with the way your plants look, plant them in the bottle. Don't crowd your garden. Remember that the plants will slowly grow and fill up the space.

8. Make holes in the soil for your plants. Gently lower the plants into the bottle and put them in their holes. Pat the soil down firmly around the base of each plant.

9. If you wish, you can add some small decorations in among the plants — maybe a shell or a little piece of driftwood.

10. Water the garden. It should be moist but *not* soaked. Put the lid in place. As long as the lid is on, your garden will need only a few drops of water every month or so.

11. Water your garden lightly, *only* if the soil seems dry. If the glass fogs up with water, your bottle garden has been watered too much. Take the lid off for a couple of days to let it dry out.

12. Put your bottle garden where it gets light. Don't put it in direct sunlight.

Flowers:
Plants' Advertising

*F*lowers add color and beauty to our lives. They come in many shapes and sizes. They can be almost any color but black. (Some are such a dark purple that they *look* black.) Flowers delight our noses as well as our eyes. In fact, many perfumes are made from flowers.

Flowering plants can grow just about anywhere in the world. Some flowers can grow in the desert where there's almost no water and the sun is blazing hot. Some grow in the arctic and near the tops of high mountains where they have to melt the snow before they can peek through.

In cities and towns, flowers are everywhere. People plant them in parks, in their own gardens, in windowboxes and in hanging pots. Other flowers grow all by themselves — in fields, in vacant lots and even in sidewalk cracks.

But why do plants make flowers? It isn't just to please us. Flowers are busy workshops that make the plant's seeds. Many flowers need insects (and sometimes even birds, bats or rats) to help them with their work.

Your parents might pay you to set the table or walk the dog. A plant "pays" insects for their work too — with pollen and nectar. The colorful flower and the sweet scent of the nectar are the plant's ways of advertising that it has things insects want.

We probably notice a flower's brightly colored petals first — and insects do too. Some flowers, like pansies, have several petals in a circle.

Some, like morning glories, have one petal that forms a funnel or tube. Petals give insects who visit a flower a place to land. Sometimes petals have stripes on them. These act like runways for the insects. They guide them to the center of the flower.

Why do insects want to go to the center of the flower? To get a drink of *nectar*. Many flowers make this sweet liquid. Insects stick their long mouth parts into the center of the flower and suck up the nectar. (It's like sipping a soft drink through a straw.)

Also at the center of the flower, almost hidden by the petals, is a vase-shaped part called the *pistil*. At the bottom of the pistil are some *ovules* undeveloped seeds. Thin stalks called *stamens* are arranged around the pistil. On the end of the stamens is a yellow powder called *pollen*.

For the plant to make seeds that will grow into new plants, pollen has to fall into the pistil. The pollen joins with the ovule to make a seed. This is called *fertilization*.

Some plants depend on the wind to spread their pollen. But many of them need insects. (Some large tropical flowers use hummingbirds or bats.) As the insects drink the nectar, their bodies become coated with pollen from the stamens. When they visit the next flower some of the pollen will rub off on the sticky top of the pistil. In this way the flower is helped to make its seeds. Aren't we lucky that plants have chosen *this* way of reproducing?

❀ *BUSY, BUZZY BEES: FLOWERS' BEST FRIENDS* When you put honey on your toast, think about this: bees had to make about 80,000 trips to flowers to gather the jar of honey for you. If all these journeys were made into one, a bee could go around the world twice!

Bees visit far more flowers than other insects. A bee isn't just drinking nectar, it is storing the nectar in a honey sac inside its body. When the

POLLEN BAG

bee returns to the hive, it pours the honey into little wax boxes called *honeycombs*. The bees gather around these little boxes and vibrate their wings 400 times a second. This takes all the water out of the nectar and makes it into honey.

Bees also collect pollen to make into "bee bread." They carry the pollen back to their hives in little bags on their hind legs. If you watch bees buzzing around flowers, you can often spot the bright yellow bags of pollen on their legs. Sometimes you wonder if they will be able to take off with such a leavy load. Each bee carries thousands of pollen grains on every trip.

🌸 *PICK A THOUSAND FLOWERS* Do you think you would get tired picking a thousand flowers? Not if you pick a sunflower. What we think of as a single flower is really more than a thousand tiny flowers joined together. The plushy-looking center of the flower is made up of *disk florets*. Floret just means "little flower." Each disk floret has its own

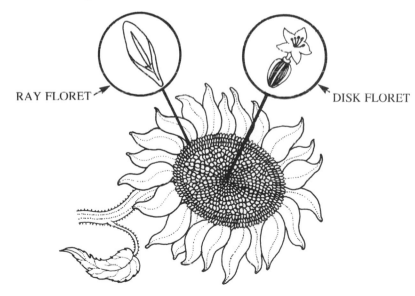

RAY FLORET

DISK FLORET

stamens and pistil and forms a seed. In a circle around the disk florets are the *ray florets*. Each of them has one petal. They don't have any seeds — their only job is to attract insects to the flower. Dandelions, daisies and lots of other flowers are also made up of many tiny florets. If you take one of these flowers apart carefully, you can see the tiny flowers all working together.

SUPER STINKER   The largest flower in the world is found in the jungles of Southeast Asia. It's called the Rafflesia. It takes five months for its spotted orangey-red flower to grow. This giant flower is about the size of a plastic wading pool — almost one metre across. It can have a mass of up to 12 kg (26 lb.). Wouldn't it be wonderful if the Rafflesia had a super perfume to match its size? Unfortunately, this flower uses flies to spread its pollen — and they are attracted by the smell of rotting meat. So that's what the Rafflesia gives them. Yuk!

Discover a Flower's Secrets

To see all the working parts of a flower clearly, you have to take it apart.

What You Need:

One of these flowers:
petunia
snapdragon
salvia
toadflax
tulip
daffodil
morning glory

(All of the flowers listed have both *stamens* and *pistils* — some other flowers don't.)

What to Do:

1. Admire the flower for a minute. Look at the way all its parts fit together. Sniff its perfume.
2. The bulging part of the stem is the *receptacle*. It holds the flower up.
3. The green flower parts just under the petals are called *sepals* (Some flowers don't have sepals.) How many are there? How are they arranged? See if you can find a flower bud of the same

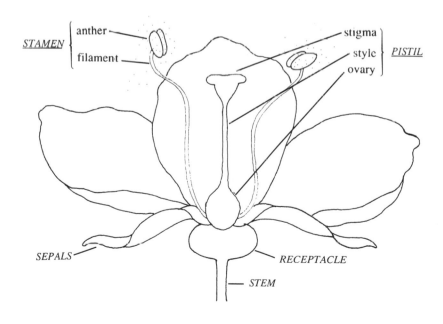

STAMEN { anther
filament

stigma
style } PISTIL
ovary

SEPALS

RECEPTACLE

STEM

kind as the flower you are taking apart. Where are the sepals on the bud? What do you think the sepals are for?

4. Next look at the petals. Where are they attached to the flower? How are they arranged? Are there any special markings that look as if they might be for bees? Where do you think insects would land on this flower? Carefully remove the petals.

5. Can you see some thin stalks sticking out of the center of the flower? These are the *stamens*. How many are there? Where are they attached to the flower? Touch the ends of the stamens. What is the fine powder called? What color is it?

6. ⊘ At the very center of the flower is a green vase-shaped part called the *pistil*. The bulging bottom part of the pistil is the *ovary*. Sometimes it is possible to split the ovary open with your thumbnail. You can also ask a grownup to cut across the ovary very carefully with a sharp knife. Can you see the *ovules* inside? (Use a magnifying glass if you have one.)

Drying Flowers

If you dry flowers carefully, you can make bouquets with them that last a long time.

What You Need:

some wildflowers such as
> tansies
> everlastings
> goldenrod
> Queen Anne's lace

or

some garden flowers such as
> sunflowers
> strawflowers
> hydrangeas

string or twist ties (from sandwich
> bags)
clothesline
clothes pegs
a dark dry place to hang the flowers

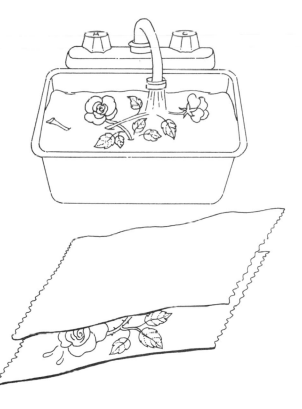

What to Do:

1. Pick the flowers on a dry day. Choose flowers that have just opened and haven't been nibbled by insects. Keep as much stem with the flowers as you can — but don't pull them up by the roots. If the stems are too tough to break, use scissors.

3. Carefully take any leaves off the stems. If you leave them on, they just crumble into powder as the flower dries.

5. Stretch the clothesline across the dark dry place where you are going to dry the flowers. Use the clothes pegs to attach the flower stems to the clothesline.

6. It will take about two weeks for the flowers to dry. When the flowers are completely dry, you can arrange them in jars and vases. Handle them carefully — they can break very easily.

4. Use string or twist ties to make flower bunches of three or four. Leave big flowers like sunflowers as single stalks.

Ask yourself: Do the dried flowers look the same as they did when they were growing? Do they feel the same? Did some of the flowers change more than others? Did some of the flowers fall apart while they were drying? Which kinds of flowers seem to dry best?

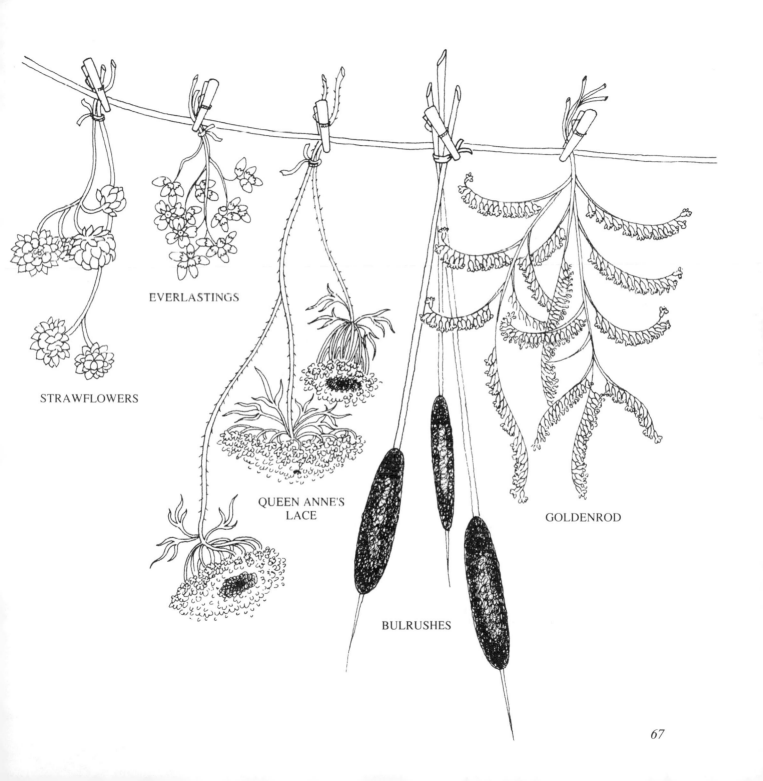

STRAWFLOWERS

EVERLASTINGS

QUEEN ANNE'S
LACE

BULRUSHES

GOLDENROD

67

A Petal Project that Makes Scents

For hundreds of years people have been using dried flowers, leaves and spices to make their houses smell sweeter and to perfume their clothing, sheets and towels. A mixture of dried flower petals is called *potpourri*.

What You Need:

assorted flowers with different
    scents (roses, peonies, mock
    orange blossoms, lilacs, lilies-of-
    the-valley, for example)
newspaper
an old window screen and 2 bricks
    or boxes
some bottles with lids
gummed labels

What to Do:

1. Gather some flowers on a dry day. Choose flowers in full bloom. (Ask permission before you pick them!)
2. Spread out the newspaper. Carefully pull the petals off the flowers. Throw out the stems, leaves and any wilted petals.
3. Spread the petals out on the screen. The petals should not touch each other. Set the screen on two bricks or two boxes so that the air can get at the petals from all sides. Put the screen in a warm dry place that is not in direct sunlight.
4. Every day for a week, turn the petals. When they feel dry and crisp they are ready to store.
5. Store each kind of petal in a separate bottle with the lid screwed on tightly. Label each bottle so you know what's inside.
6. To use the petals to scent a room, put some in an open bowl.
7. To use the petals to scent a drawer, package them like this: Put a square of cotton cloth 12 cm x 12 cm (5 sq. in.) on top of a square of net of the same size. Put a few spoonfuls of dried petals on the cloth. Gather up the cloth and the net and tie with a ribbon.

Try out different mixtures of petals. You can also mix petals with spices such as cinnamon and cloves or herbs such as mint and rosemary.

Pick a Tiny Bouquet

What You Need:

tiny "vases" (screw tops from bottles, perfume bottles, old lipstick lids or other little containers you find around the house)

What to Do:

1. Now that you've chosen a vase, you know how tiny your bouquet has to be. In your yard, in a meadow or at the park, bend down and look closely. Once you start thinking small, you'll see little flowers you don't usually pay much attention to. You might find chickweed, clover, violas or shepherd's purses. What else can you find? (Check a wildflower book to discover the names of your bouquet flowers.)

Fruits:
What Are They, Anyway?

Have you ever heard two kids having an argument about tomatoes? It usually goes something like this:

FIRST KID: "You know what? I just found out that a tomato is a fruit."

SECOND KID: "You're crazy — a tomato is a vegetable! Whoever heard of tomato jam or tomato ice cream?"

You can understand why the second kid doesn't believe the first one. In everyday life, we use the word "vegetable" for plant food that we eat in our salads or during the main course of our meals. Usually vegetables are not as sweet as fruits. We don't eat vegetables for dessert.

The word *vegetable* doesn't tell you anything about the part of the plant the food comes from. A carrot is a root, celery is a stem, lettuce is a leaf. And a tomato is a fruit.

A fruit is simply the part of the plant that contains the seeds. Apples, oranges and strawberries are fruits — but so are peanuts, cucumbers, green beans and pumpkins. They all have seeds inside them. Not all fruits can be eaten — at least by human beings. A milkweed pod is a fruit and so is a cotton boll. Can you think of some others?

Fruits grow out of flowers. Can you guess which part of the flower becomes the fruit? When you looked at the parts of a flower, you found the ovules that would become seeds. They were inside the ovary (the rounded bottom part of the pistil). Have you guessed it now? The ovary gets bigger and bigger and becomes the fruit. Most of the other flower parts dry up and drop off the plant.

Some fruits, like peaches and cherries and many kinds of nuts, contain just one big seed. Others, like oranges, tomatoes and milkweed pods, have many seeds inside them. If you've ever helped to carve a Hallowe'en Jack-O-Lantern, you know that a pumpkin has hundreds of seeds in it.

Seeds are arranged in many interesting ways inside fruits. Carefully take apart bean pods and look at the way the seeds are attached. Can you see any little ovules that were not fertilized? If you cut an apple lengthwise (ask a grownup to help you), you can easily see the ovary with the seeds inside it.

If there are any flowering plants where you live, you can watch the flowers change into fruits over the growing season. You have to be patient to watch this magic show put on by nature. It happens a lot more slowly than pulling a rabbit out of a hat — but it's just as interesting!

❀ EXPLODING FRUIT What will go through the air like speeding bullets? These are the seeds from the exploding fruit of the wild cucumber, hurtling through the air at 100 km/h (60 mph). The outside of the fruit is prickly and tough. The inside is juicy and becomes more and more swollen as the seeds develop. Finally, the inside of the fruit pushes so hard against the outside that the fruit explodes. The seeds zoom up to 7 m (20 ft.) away from the parent plant.

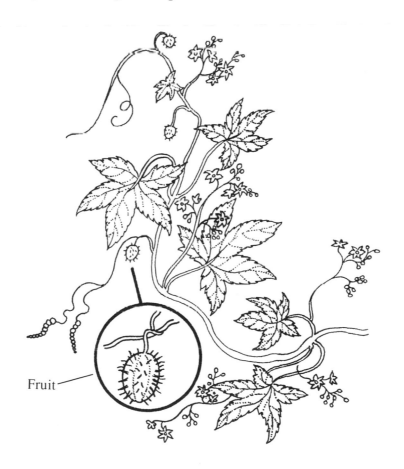

Fruit

What's Inside a Fruit?

Take a look at some different kinds of fruits and the seeds inside them. Remember that many vegetables are called fruits by scientists because they are seed containers.

What You Need:

5 or 6 different fruits such as apples, squash, bean pods, tomatoes, oranges, grapes or cucumbers
knife
tray
paper towels
magnifying glass

What to Do:

1. Spread some paper towels on a tray to make a place to work.
2. Take a close look at the fruits you chose. Can you tell which end of the fruit was attached to the plant? Can you see any flower parts still on the fruit?
3. ⊘ Cut open the fruits. Can you see where the ovary and ovules were in the flower?
4. Look at the way the seeds are arranged. How many seeds does each fruit have? (Some fruits have so many seeds that you can't count all of them. Count the seeds in one section and make a guess about the number of seeds in the whole fruit.) Why do you think some fruits have so few seeds and some have so many?
5. Save the seeds from each fruit. Wash the seeds with water — don't use soap! Put them in a warm place to dry. Plant a couple of seeds from each kind of fruit in some soil to see if they will grow. Water them lightly. (As a planter, you could use an egg carton with a little soil in each section.)

Many of the leftovers from this activity make tasty snacks. Happy munching!

Fruit Prints

When you cut a fruit in half, you will find a beautiful design of seeds and sections inside. Many of these designs can be saved by using the fruit to make prints.

What You Need:

knife
apples, oranges, lemons
poster paints
tinfoil pie plate
white drawing paper

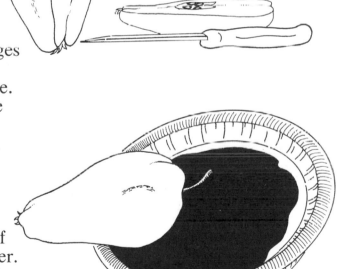

What to Do:

1. ⊘ Cut a fruit in half. Cut oranges and lemons through their middles. Cut apples lengthwise.
2. Pour some poster paint into the pie plate. Pour just enough to cover the bottom of the plate. Tilt the plate until it is evenly covered with paint.
3. Press the cut side of the fruit into the paint.
4. Press the paint-covered side of the fruit onto the drawing paper. Be very careful not to move the fruit as you make your print. (If you move the fruit, your print will smear.)

5. Carefully lift the fruit and see a beautiful design. Can you see where the seeds were stored inside the fruit?

If you have some large sheets of paper, you can make a repeat design to use as gift wrap.

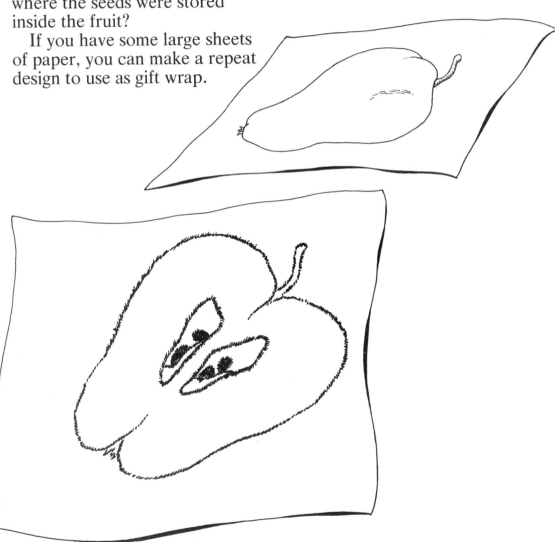

Seeds: Special Delivery Packages

Human babies grow protected and fed inside their mother's bodies for nine months. Baby plants are sent off by their parent plants long before they are ready to start growing on their own. How do baby plants set off on their journey? How can they survive alone? It's all done with seeds.

All flowering plants make fruits with seeds inside them. As we saw, some fruits — like tomatoes—contain many seeds. Some — like peaches — contain just one seed. Each seed is a well-wrapped package. Inside is a tiny baby plant — called an *embryo* — and some food to help it grow. The hard outer coat of the seed protects the baby plant on its travels.

Before a seed can sprout into a new plant, it has to land on the ground. And it needs room to grow. If the new plant is too close to its parent, they will have to fight each other for food and water. So plants have invented lots of ways to spread their seeds.

Some plants send their seed packages by air. Maple seeds look like spinning helicopter blades as they flutter down from the tree on a pair of papery wings. Dandelion seeds and milkweed seeds are attached to silky white tufts that act like parachutes. The lightest breeze carries them along and sets them down far away. (It's much easier to blow dandelion seeds away than it is to blow out all your birthday candles!)

Other plants depend on birds and animals to deliver their seeds for them. You've probably seen busy squirrels burying seeds and nuts. They're storing up food for later on but they won't find everything they've hidden. The uneaten nuts and seeds can grow into new plants. When birds and animals eat fruit, the hard seeds pass right through their bodies without being harmed. The seeds come out in their droppings — far from the parent plant and fertilized too!

Some plants don't have tasty fruits or seeds that animals want to eat. Their seeds — called *burrs* — simply hitch a ride. Burrs are covered with little hooks that catch in the fur of passing animals. As you've likely found out, burrs will also stick in socks, sweaters and mittens. A plant was using *you* to spread its seeds.

After a seed falls to the ground, it may sleep for some time. Many seeds stay asleep for the winter. In spring, when the sun warms the soil and rainwater makes it moist, the seed can begin to grow. This is called *germination*.

Water enters the seed and makes it swell. Inside the seed, the little embryo begins to grow and use its food supply. The hard outer coat cracks and the first little root pushes its way out. This root begins to take in more water and minerals from the soil. The first stem makes its way up out of the soil and into the sunlight. When it sprouts its first green leaves, it can begin to make food for itself. A new plant has begun its life.

✿ *SEEDS THAT LIVED FOR 10,000 YEARS*   Some ancient seeds of the Arctic Lupin plant were found frozen in the Yukon in 1954. Scientists believed they were between 10,000 and 15,000 years old. Some of them sprouted and grew into plants. One even had some flowers on it!

✿ *GIANT SEEDS*   Some of the largest seeds in the world come from a palm called the *Coco de Mer* ("coconut of the sea"). It grows on the Seychelles Islands in the Indian Ocean. Coco de Mer seeds may grow bigger than beachballs and weigh as much as 23 kg (51 lb.). These giant seeds are also long-distance travellers. They float in the ocean from one island to another. Long ago, people who found these seeds on their beaches thought they came from underwater trees.

✿ *SEEDS THAT LOVE A FIRE*   The Lodgepole Pine and the Knobcone Pine need a forest fire before they can spread their seeds! Their tough cones — with seeds inside — can stay closed and attached to the trees for years. It takes the fierce heat of a fire to pop open their cones. In this way, a forest that was destroyed by a fire can soon be reseeded with new little pine trees.

What's Inside a Seed?

What You Need:

dried lima beans
a magnifying glass
a jar or glass
water

What to Do:

1. Look closely at the dried lima bean. Can you take off its outer coating? Can you break it open?
2. Put two or three lima beans in a jar. Cover them with water and leave them to soak for a day.
3. Remove the beans from the water. Are they still the same size?
4. Take a look at the outside of a bean. What is its coating like now? Can you see where the lima bean (seed) used to be attached to the pod (the fruit)? Just above this point is a tiny hole where water enters the fruit.
5. Peel off the outer coat of the seed. Using your fingernail, carefully break the seed into two halves.
6. Can you see the seed's food supply? Can you see the baby plant (the embryo)? Which takes up more space inside the plant, the baby plant or its food?
7. If you have a magnifying glass, take a closer look at the baby plant. The lower, hook-shaped part of the embryo will become the root of the new plant. The little leaf-shaped part will become the stem and the first two leaves.

Try soaking seeds of other kinds and looking inside them.

How Far Do Seeds Travel?

This is something to do outdoors on a dry day.

What You Need:

a chair
some winged tree seeds, like maple
   and ash seeds
dandelion heads at the fluffy stage
a long tape measure

What to Do:

I. TREE SEEDS

1. Place the chair outside. Choose an open place where the wind can carry the seeds.
2. Stand down on the chair and throw a winged seed up in the air. Watch it as it sails through the air. Notice where it comes down.
3. Use the tape measure to find out how far it travelled.
4. Try it again with another seed. Which seeds go the farthest?
5. Now tear the wings off one or two of the seeds. How far do they go when you throw them up in the air?

II. DANDELION SEEDS

1. Count the seeds on a dandelion head. Now blow on the head. How many blows does it take to blow away all the seeds?
2. Use the tape measure to find out how far the seeds travelled.
3. Wet the parachutes of a couple of seeds with some water. Try blowing them away. Will they still float through the air? What kind of weather do you think would be best for a dandelion that is scattering its seeds?

Crowding Isn't Healthy

Have you ever been in a very crowded place — maybe it was a full bus or streetcar — where your toes were being stepped on and you were being pushed and elbowed? Most people don't like to be crowded together like this. Plants don't like it either. Find out for yourself what happens when seeds are planted too close together.

What You Need:

6 waxed cardboard milk cartons
scissors
package of marigold or mustard
    seeds
potting soil

What to Do:

1. ⊘ Cut one long side panel off each carton. Punch three or four small holes in the other side.
2. Fill each carton with damp soil.
3. In the first carton, make small holes in the soil about 1 cm (½ in.) deep. (Use a pencil or your finger.) Make the holes about 8 cm (3 in.) apart. Put two seeds in each hole. Gently refill the holes with soil.
4. In each of the other cartons, plant the seeds closer and closer together: at 6.5 cm, 5 cm, 3.5 cm, 2 cm and 1 cm (2½ in., 2 in., 1½ in., 1 in., ½ in.).
5. Put the cartons in a warm sunlit place. Keep the cartons lightly watered. As the seedlings begin to push through, be sure not to let the soil dry out or the seedlings will die.
6. There should be only one seedling in each hole. If two come up, pull one out.
7. About two weeks after planting, each plant will have several leaves. Compare the plants in the six cartons. Are there differences in height? In which carton did the plants grow the tallest? In which carton are the plants the leafiest? Which ones look the healthiest to you? Which look the least healthy? What

distance apart do you think your seeds should be planted?

Here's something else to think about: Did all the seeds you planted germinate (sprout)? Did all of the seedlings that came up grow into plants? Does this tell you something about why plants make so many seeds?

SOMETHING TO DO

A Sticky Adventure

Suppose you are a burr. You attach yourself to a passing rabbit or dog — or maybe you get stuck to a person. Make up a story about your travels. You can write about your adventure, make it into a comic strip, draw a picture of it or just tell it to someone.

Trees:
Giants of the
Plant World

What would the world be like without trees? It would be a lot less pleasant for all of us. We would certainly miss the beauty of the trees. In the spring and summer, their rustling leaves form a bright green canopy over our heads. In the autumn, many trees stage a dazzling leaf show in red, orange and yellow. Even in winter, bare black branches swaying in the wind make interesting patterns against the sky. The evergreens, of course, add their rich green to our neighborhoods all year round.

A summer without trees would be hotter — and dirtier. Trees give us shade and coolness on a hot summer day. In fact, trees act like giant air conditioners. Even when the ground is dry and sandy, a tree is able to find traces of water. A large tree might pump up 900 L (over 200 gal.) of water from the ground on a hot day. (That's enough water to fill your bathtub four times.) Some of the water is given off by the leaves of the tree and cools the air. Trees are also busy cleaning the air. They take carbon dioxide (which is poisonous to us) out of the air and use it to make food.

A world without trees would leave many animals homeless — and foodless. Birds, small animals such as squirrels and mice and many kinds of insects make their homes in trees. Just about every part of the tree — fruit, nuts, leaves, bark — provides food for some living creature.

Trees cover about one-third of the earth's land surface. Trees are the biggest plants on earth — and the oldest. In fact, these giants live *much* longer than we do. No human being every lived to be older than 117. But trees can live for hundreds of years — and some kinds live for thousands.

Trees, like many other plants, grow from seeds. Their roots grow deep into the soil, searching for water and keeping the tree from being blown over. Usually the roots of a tree spread about as widely under the ground as the branches of the tree spread in the air.

Tree stems are different from the stems of other plants. Green stems die at the end of each growing season. But tree stems (usually called *trunks*) keep growing from year to year. Look around your neighborhood to see if you can find a large tree that has been cut down. You can learn about the way trees grow by looking at the flat surface of the stump.

On the outside of the trunk is a rough coat called the bark. It protects the tender growing parts of the tree. Just inside the bark is the *cambium,* where new tree trunk is growing. In the spring, when the tree grows faster, the new wood being formed is light-colored. At the end of the growing season, when the tree grows more slowly, the new wood is darker. The ring of light and dark wood shows one year of the tree's growth. The cambium layer of the trunk carries food made by the leaves to all parts of the tree.

The next layer in from the cambium is called the *sapwood*. The living sapwood carries water and minerals up from the roots to the rest of the tree. Depending on how old the tree is, the sapwood will show many growth rings. At the very center of the tree is a hard dead core called *heartwood*. It no longer carries any food or water but it makes the tree strong.

Each year, some of the sapwood closest to the heartwood becomes heartwood, making the heart of the tree stronger and thicker. The ring formed by the cambium becomes the outer ring of sapwood, and a new layer of cambium grows. You will stop growing at around the age of eighteen. But a tree keeps getting larger and larger, adding rings to its trunk, for as long as it lives.

THE WORLD'S OLDEST LIVING TREE The world's oldest living tree is nicknamed "Methuselah," after the person in the Bible who lived the longest. It's a Bristlecone Pine, a twisted gnarled little tree that grows in the White Mountains of California. This tree is over 4600 years old. In the early 1960s, an older bristlecone pine was growing in California — it was about 4900 years old — but it was cut down with a chainsaw to find its age! You might be wondering how a tree can be dated *without* cutting it down. People who study trees use a tiny hollow drill to bore a hole into the centre of the tree trunk. Then they remove a thin core of wood — and count the rings on it.

✿ *THE BACKWARDS BANYAN* We expect a tree to root itself in the ground and work its way up. But the banyan tree of India has it all backwards. It sends out roots from its *branches* which have to work their way down. When they finally root themselves in the ground, they become thick and woody like extra trunks. The branches of the banyan just keep getting longer and longer, sending down more and more roots to prop them up. Some large banyans have as many as 350 prop roots — so that one tree looks like a small forest.

THE BIGGEST LIVING THING ON EARTH   The biggest living thing on earth is not an elephant. It's not a whale, either. It's a Sequoia tree in California, nicknamed "General Sherman." Its trunk is over 24 m (almost 80 ft.) around. That means it would take more than thirty children, linking hands, to reach all the way around it. This tree has a mass of over 2030 tonnes (just under 2000 tons). There's enough wood in it to build about forty houses — or to make 5,000,000,000 matches.

Your Own Special Tree

Somewhere near where you live is a tree that is going to become "your tree" for a whole year. Maybe you can see it from your window. Maybe you pass it on the way to school or to a friend's house. Start watching this tree today. Here are some ideas to get you started.

What You Need:

a notebook or scrapbook

What to Do:

1. Find out what kind of tree it is. Ask its owner or look in a library book about trees. Give your tree a special name.
2. Make some drawings of your tree or take some photographs. How does it look in the winter? In the summer?
3. What kind of leaves does it have? Collect a leaf (just *one*) in the spring, the summer, and the fall. Press them (see p. 45). What kind of seeds does it have? Collect some that have fallen to the ground.
4. Measure your tree. How big around is it? (Use a tape measure or measure with a hug — can you put your arms right around it?) How tall is your tree? Taller than you? Taller than a two-storey house? (See page 90 for a way to measure its height.)
5. Do birds and animals visit your tree? What kinds? Where in the tree do they like to sit? Are there any nests in your tree?
6. Are there any insects on the trunk and leaves of your tree? Can you find out what they are? (Use books at the library to find out.)
7. Put the big events in your tree's life in your notebook. On what day did you first see buds on its branches? On what day did its leaves begin to fall (if it's a tree that loses its leaves)? When were its branches completely bare? Were there any big storms that affected your tree (covering it with ice, making it bend and sway, maybe knocking off twigs or even branches)?

How Tall Is That Tree?

You don't have to carry your tape measure to the top of a tree to measure how tall it is! Here is a useful trick you can use to measure trees and other tall things too.

What You Need:

a partner to work with
a pencil
a tape measure or ruler

What to Do:

1. Find a tall tree that is standing on fairly flat ground.
2. Back up from the tree. Stop when you are farther away from the tree than the base of the tree is from its top. (If the tree were lying on the ground, it wouldn't quite reach you.)
3. Ask your partner to stand right at the tree (picture 1).
4. Hold a pencil straight up and down as shown in picture 1. Grasp it near its end. Close one eye and hold the pencil so that it lines up with the tree.
5. Move forward or backward until the part of the pencil above your thumb looks like it is as tall as the tree.

PICTURE 1

6. Carefully turn the pencil sideways keeping your thumb lined up with the tree trunk. Your pencil should now look like it is lying along the ground (picture 2).

7. Ask your partner to walk away from the tree. It will seem as if your partner is walking along the pencil. Tell your partner to stop when she or he is lined up with the end of the pencil.

8. Measure the distance from the base of the tree to the place where your partner is standing. This is about the height of the tree.

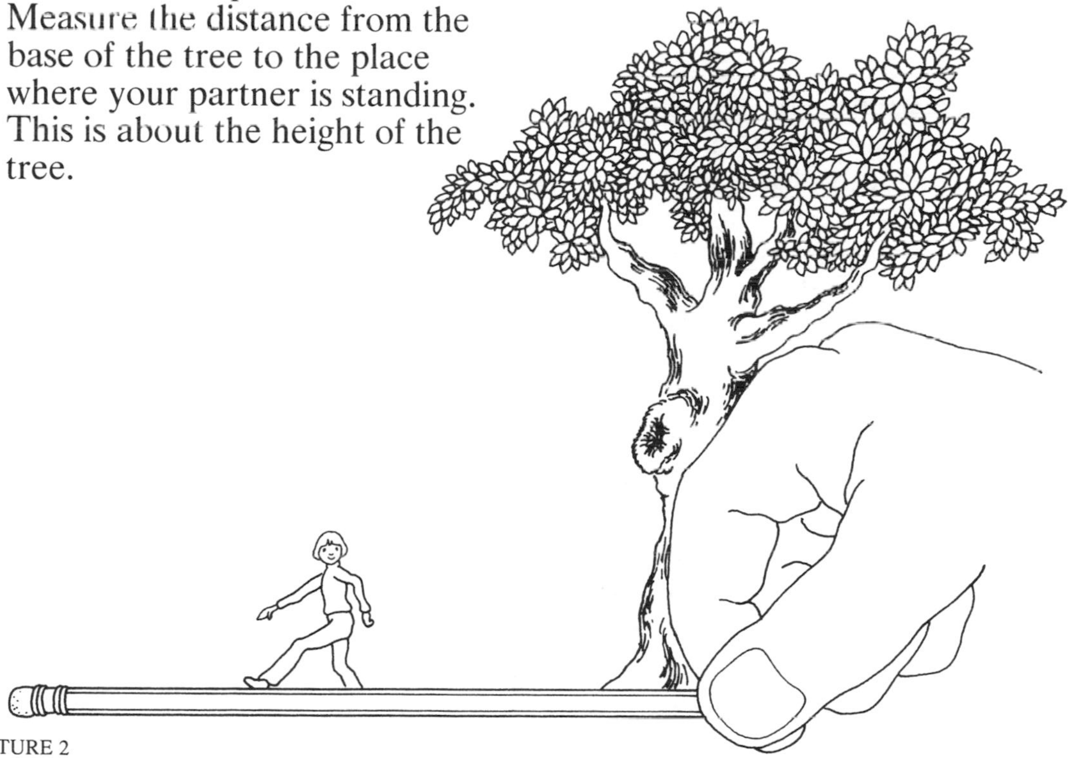

PICTURE 2

Stumps Tell a Story

If you come upon a dry tree stump, you can take a rubbing that will tell you the tree's life story.

What You Need:

shelf paper, computer printout
   paper or other paper big enough
   to stretch across the tree trunk
thumb tacks
charcoal (get at an art supply store)

What to Do:

1. Stretch the paper across the stump. Hold it in place with thumb tacks. Make sure the paper can't move.
2. Use the side of the piece of charcoal to rub across the paper. Rub in just *one* direction across the stump.
3. Soon the tree rings and other marks on your stump will show through on your paper. When you are satisfied with your rubbing, take it off the stump.
4. While you are still at the stump, mark the center of the tree on your rubbing. Count off the rings and mark every tenth year. (If anything is unclear on your rubbing, you can check it on the stump.)

Here's what to look for to reveal your tree's story

1. The number of rings tells you hold old the tree was when it was cut down. (If you also know when the tree was cut down, you can figure out when it began to grow. Can you find the year of your birth on the tree's rings?)
2. Look at the growth rings. Are some of them wider than usual? These probably show years when there was lots of rain. Are some of them narrow? These may have been dry years.
3. Was the tree growing evenly in all directions? If it grew more on one side than the other, can you see any reasons for it? For example, was the tree crowded on one side by a building or another tree?

4. If the tree is old, it might
be interesting to discover what
things were like when it began to
grow. Perhaps it is in the middle
of the city now, but twenty-five
or fifty years ago, it may have
been in a field or a forest. See
if you can find out.

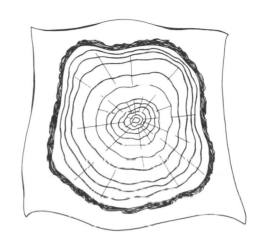

Bark Rubbings

What You Need:

thin sheets of white paper
wax crayons
masking tape

What to Do:

1. Find a tree with interesting markings on its bark. (Maybe it's your "adopted" tree!)
2. Use masking tape to tape the paper to the tree.
3. Take the paper wrapping off a crayon. Rub the side of the crayon over the paper until the markings on the bark show up clearly on the paper.

Index